TOUCHING THE GOD
OF
JACOB

By Dennis Paul Goldsworthy-Davis

Open Wells Ministries

15315 Capital Port

San Antonio, TX 78249

www.openwellsministries.org

Library of Congress Number:

ISBN: 978-0-9979192-8-8

Printed in the United States of America by Open Wells Ministries

TABLE OF CONTENTS

Jacob was a man who had many encounters with God.
Starting with his encounter at Bethel where his grandfather
Abraham had built an altar, he experienced many places
where God intervened in his life to fulfill God's will
through him and the budding nation of Israel. The Lord had
to fulfill His covenant with Abraham and produce a nation
to bring forth the Messiah. This could not be done without
Jacob becoming who he needed to be. This is so often true
of us as well. We are necessary to the purposes of God. Yet
in our natural state we are incapable of agreeing with the
Lord so what He desires and needs can be accomplished.
He has to fashion us into what is necessary to His will
being done. This is what the times and places of encounter
were about in Jacob's life. The Lord is the master
craftsman. He knows how to form us. Isaiah 43:1 echoes
this idea.

But now, thus says the Lord, who created you,
O Jacob, And He who formed you, O Israel:
"Fear not, for I have redeemed you; I have
called you by your name; You are Mine.
Jacob was created but Israel was formed. This is because
Jacob and Israel are the same. We see God changing the

name of Jacob to Israel in Genesis 32:28 after an all-night wrestling match.

And He said, "Your name shall no longer be called Jacob, but Israel; for you have struggled with God and with men, and have prevailed."

He was born Jacob but was fashioned into Israel by the handiwork of God. We are designed to be His workmanship according to Ephesians 2:10.

For we are His workmanship, created in Christ Jesus for good works, which God prepared beforehand that we should walk in them.

The word *workmanship* is the Greek word *poiema*. It means *a product or something made*. It is the idea of a *piece of art*. The Greek word *poiema* is what we get our word *poem* from. God takes us in our natural state and through encounters with Him, we become His work of art or masterpiece. This is what happened with Jacob. He started off in the natural as Jacob but became Israel, a prince of God. Every time we have an encounter with the presence and glory of God, we receive another dimension of grace. This grace is what fashions and transforms us into that which is necessary to the God's purposes. We are moved from who we are naturally to who we are meant to be supernaturally.

In this book *'Touching the God of Jacob"* my good friend, Dennis Goldsworthy-Davis unveils and unlocks this idea and others. Dennis writes from a wealth of experience of encounters with God. He understands not just from a theological place, but a lifetime of walking with God, what touching and being touched by God does in a person's life. This is why he is so jealous for this in his life, but also desires to see it unlocked in yours as well. I believe this book will do just that.

Robert Henderson Best-Selling Author, *"The Court of Heaven"* Series

INTRODUCTION

I have been in the ministry for many years and a preacher for all but two of those years. I suddenly had the Lord speak something to me that did not make sense with my personal knowledge of scripture. It was a **Sunday** morning and I had been waiting for the word of the Lord to preach that morning. Silence was all I heard. Absolutely nothing. Time was rushing on! Oh no, not one of those mornings! One of those mornings when it would be a last-minute revelation, a just-before-you-get-up-to-preach revelation. It does not matter how long you have preached, this can be a little stressful. Even though inspirational, I like to prepare the word. Of course I do. So it looked like he was holding me again to the last minute. I got up from the table where I was sitting and, in frustration, went to get a cup of coffee. The usual prayers had been prayed. There was the confession of all and everything that might have blocked my hearing. I offered to let one of the other team members preach. But nothing! Oh, he had my attention alright! I was resigning myself to the obvious last-minute word. I think my heart rate had just started to go up, but as I walked back to the table the Lord said something to me. Something that made me stop and question him. He said, "The God of Jacob.".

"The God of Jacob?", I questioned. "That's not right.", I said. The scripture says, "The God of Abraham, Isaac and Jacob."

I heard it again, "The God of Jacob." Now he had my attention. I opened my concordance and there it was! Mainly in the Psalms and then in Micah and Isaiah and even mentioned in the book of Acts. Wow! How can you study the word so much and miss something like this? Quite simply because it was awaiting an appointed time in your life and ministry. The God of Jacob! Why the separation from Abraham and Isaac? What did the Lord want to show me? Why since that day has it come back and back and back. Why did David mention it so much? What hidden gems of revelation and encounter were hidden in this one statement? It has held me in such continued thirst and longing that I felt it would be good to write this book to perhaps open up some of my revelations to others that they, too could experience the Lord like Jacob did and more so, because we have the Christ.

THE FACE OF GOD

Let's start with a bang! What is Jacob famous for? Many things but perhaps the most famous of all is his Genesis 32 wrestle with God. He makes this statement

> *"I have seen God face to face and yet lived."*
> Genesis 32:30

 I HAVE SEEN GOD FACE TO FACE! Didn't God tell Moses that he could see his glory but not see his face?

> *"[You cannot see my face and live]."* Exodus 33:20

But Jacob did! Abraham talked with him as a friend according to Isaiah and so did Moses but...face to face? Why is this experience so relevant to revelation on the God of Jacob? Because there is a scripture that the Lord used to awaken me to the whole revelation and it involves you and me. It is found in Psalms. It follows the description of intimacy with God and suddenly David lets this bombshell of a statement out,

> *"Such is the generation of those that seek his face, your face oh God of Jacob."* Psalms 24:6

A generation that would have a face to face encounter with God! But listen to the second statement, *"YOUR FACE"*, David had encountered the same face to face that Jacob had! Yes, he was prophesying of a generation. I believe the redeemed generation. But then he lets us all know he had, just as Jacob, encountered the face of God.

Firstly, this is the first time David mentions the God of Jacob, which means this is the introduction to the great revelation. But what an introduction. He is saying he met God the way Jacob did. God manifested to him the way he manifested to Jacob! But also, David stepped into a New Testament experience that belonged to the redeemed. Listen to what he says:

> *"The Lord said to my Lord."* Psalm 110:1

"My Lord"? He saw Jesus before he came. He encountered and surrendered to the King. It must have been face to face! He is the one that says,

> *"Restore to me the joy of your salvation."*
> Psalm 51:12

This is incredible. He lived under the law but knew salvation. He says,

"You have shown to me the paths of life and in your presence is the fullness of joy and at your right hand there are pleasures for ever more."
Psalm 16:11

He had stepped into the New Testament! That's why his worship and tabernacle are so relevant today. Jacob touched something, then David touched it and so can we. The way Jacob encountered God is the way the New Testament church can encounter him.

But we would be remiss to not dwell on the statement that David makes,

> *"Such is the generation of those that seek his face, your face oh God of Jacob."* Psalms 24:6

It was Jacob seeking the blessing and face of God that brought that great encounter. The Holy Spirit, like a dove, draws us to the face of God! Paul spoke of it.

> *"I want to know him, I press in to know him, I reach out to know him."* Philippians 3:10-14

Jacob was the first. He was followed by many Patriarchs but it is our privilege and joy to follow them.

JACOB THE NONCONFORMIST

Religion demands that we conform to its rules but those who make history are often the non-conformists...the rule stretchers. The boundary movers that push the limits. Jacob was no different to this. He was one of the originators of non-conformism. We see it first in the womb in the description of the wrestle between the two brothers and God's word of two nations in Genesis 25 22-25. We see it again in how he tricked his brother of his birthright in Genesis 25 29-34. Later we see it again when he pretended to be his brother and stole the fathers blessing in Genesis 27. He so desired the blessing that he definitely stretched the rules but it is later in his life that intrigues me particularly.

Jacob arrives in the east near Harran, the home of Laban his Uncle and Rebekah's brother in Genesis 29. This is just after his first real encounter with God in Genesis 28. Only God knows all that happened in that incredible encounter but he was forever changed, seeing perhaps for the first time the heavenly perspective of things. He arrives to see religion and control in full swing! In Genesis 29:2-10, Jacob arrives at a well but finds that when the need to water the sheep is apparent the "RULES" had to be obeyed. "We do it this way and that is what we do." We see this in Genesis 29:7-8. Religion makes its rules but thirst will break through. It is in verse 10 that Rachael turns up and at the sight of Rachel, Jacob rolls the stone away on his own and waters the sheep.

The story is awesome and the nature of Jacob and who he was comes to light. He never was a conformist. He didn't always do it the right way but broke through the system and water was released to family and the needy. Oh, how like the pilgrim fathers of America who paved the way for so many great things in God. Obstacles and stones are removed when there is a Jacob who wants to touch his God and wants to bless his family and minister to the needs of others. Jesus shouts out with a loud voice on the last day of the feast,

> *"On the last and greatest day of the festival, Jesus stood and said in a loud voice, 'Let anyone who is thirsty come to me and drink. Whoever believes in me, as Scripture has said, rivers of living water will flow from within them.'."* John 7:37-38.

I AM LOOKING FOR THE THIRSTY, NOT THE RELIGIOUS. The God of Jacob is touched by our thirst. We have got to break through the crowd and its religion and drink at the well.

The story of Jacob touching his God becomes a story of Jacob carrying the blessing of his God. The same God is touched in John 7 and means that a life that is touched is also a life that is carried. "Living water will flow.' Jesus, though fulfilling the law, brought a new way. Jacob brought a new way. David, when building the tabernacle of David, brought a new way. The God of Jacob broke open the way but is looking for those who will break open the way, too.

> *"The One who breaks open the way will go up before them; they will break through the gate and go out. Their King will pass through before them, the Lord at their head."* Micah 2:13

BORN SECOND

In Israel, the same as many Eastern nations, there was a special inheritance given to the first born. It was often called "the rights of the first born". They were given a double portion of the inheritance…twice what others would get. Deuteronomy 21:15-17 shows this clearly. They often would take over the family business and administrate on behalf of the father and mother. Jacob himself speaking to Rueben his firstborn said,

> *"Reuben, you are my firstborn, my might, the first sign of my strength, excelling in honor, excelling in power."* Genesis 49:3

Being first born was a place of privilege and honor higher than the other siblings. Jacob was not firstborn! But even in the womb he wrestled with his brother wanting to be. Gen 25:22-26, shows this wrestle and he even grasped his brother's heel as he was born first. So even in the womb, there was a desire to touch the blessing that ultimately came from God!

Who put such a desire in a baby in the womb? A desire which manifested all the way through his life, cheating his brother out of his birthright and stealing his blessing from his aging father as the story is told in Genesis 25 and 27. No one is saying that his methods were right. No, but his desire was so intense that, without having encountered the Lord yet personally, he tried everything within him to gain that which he felt was his. What an incredible example to those called of God to wrestle and seek to gain that which is in God for them. David himself was born number eight yet gained an inheritance that his firstborn brother never saw. Perhaps that was due to the fact he had encountered the "God of Jacob" early on in his life.

Jacob was able to touch a far greater inheritance even than his first born brother due **to desire. David was able to do the same and gain an inheritance surpassing all his** brothers! We as children of God, are given an inheritance in the firstborn himself, Christ.

> *"Now if we are children, then we are heirs – heirs of God and co-heirs with Christ, if indeed we share in his sufferings in order that we may also share in his glory".* Romans 8:17

Jesus gained the inheritance for us but when we receive him he gives us the authority to become those sons!

"Yet to all who did receive him, to those who believed in his name, he gave the right to become children of God." John 1:12

But we must, like Jacob, intensely seek it, wrestle to gain it and get the attention of the God of Jacob. I always feel that when we read that scripture in John 1:12, it really means that he opened the door to sonship. Now go and discover the land. Grasp the inheritance for yourself. How? Firstly, by the help of the Holy Spirit. Secondly by seeking the face of the God of Jacob. Thirdly, we have a great example of Paul in the New Testament.

Not that I have already obtained all this, or have already arrived at my goal, but I press on to take hold of that for which Crist Jesus took hold of me." Philippians 3:12

Wow! Paul was a New Testament Jacob touched by God for inheritance and then pursuing it with everything within him. We must pursue, pursue, pursue until we have that which is in our hearts to have. As Jacob so rightly said to the Lord,

"...I will not let you go unless you bless me." Genesis 32:26.

He got God's attention! So can we, which so many including myself can attest to!

THE GOD OF PRESENCE

What Jacob found and later on so did David is that God is a God of presence and personal touch. The Lord revealed himself to Jacob. When he did Jacob cried out,

> *"How awesome is this place! The Lord is in this place and I was not aware of it!"*
> Genesis 28:16-17

The Lord revealed his presence to Jacob! Now listen to David!

> *"You fill me with joy in your presence."*
> Psalm 16:11

In fact, David makes this statement:

> *"Tremble earth at the presence of the Lord, at the presence of the God of Jacob."*
> Psalm 114:7

The God of Jacob is a presence revealing God! The God who walked in the garden with Adam and then walked with Enoch reveals himself to Jacob and David and to any that want to know this God of Jacob.

Jacob had an encounter with the God of presence, David lived for his presence and now in the New Testament church we have the joy of the abiding presence and fellowship with the Holy Spirit. Jacob drew his presence because he longed to walk in his blessing! David drew his presence because he had a heart that was ravished for God. The prophet Samuel, speaking to Saul, said of David,

> *"But now your kingdom will not endure; the Lord has sought out a man after his own heart and appointed him ruler of his people, ..."*
> 1 Samuel 13:14

Today we are given the presence as part of our inheritance.

> *"I keep asking that the God of our Lord Jesus Christ, the glorious Father, may give you the Spirit of wisdom and revelation, so that you may know him better. I pray that the eyes of your heart may be enlightened in order that you may know the hope to which he has called you, the riches of his glorious inheritance in his holy people. And his incomparably great power for us who believe."*
> Ephesians 1, 17-19.

The presence in the form of the Holy Spirit sent by Jesus is ours according to John.

> *"And I will ask the Father, and he will give you another advocate to help you and be with you forever..."* John 14:16

The fellowship with such presence is our choice. The statement made is quite simple.

> *"If there be any fellowship."* Philippians 2:1

The God of Jacob is a God of presence! The God of Jacob revealed his presence to David. The God of Jacob wants to reveal his presence to us and walk with us in a constant fellowship.

In the book of James we are given a wonderful promise. In fact, the New King James Version states it best,

> *"Draw near to God and he will draw near to you."* James 4:8.

It was constant longing that the God of Jacob's Grandfather, Abraham, and the God of his Father, Isaac, would also bless Jacob with the same blessing! Blessed with encounters and friendship and presence. I can attest that when we come near in prayer, worship and longing for his presence he draws near to us. My Christian walk is a living testimony of such encounters and blessings.

Friends, if Jacob can draw the presence of God so can the modern-day Jacobs! Same God, same presence, if the desire is the same....

WRESTLING WITH OUR DESTINY

I am not sure how many times I have found myself back in the incredible story of God wrestling with Jacob in Genesis 32: 24-31. But it would be fair to say multiple times.

Let's look at the account slightly differently!

Firstly, it is imperative to see who started the wrestle!
"Man wrestled with Jacob." Genesis 32:24

The Lord stirred the desire and then started the wrestle. A wrestle for what? A wrestle of Destiny! He wrestled until daybreak! The dawning of a new arena in Jacobs life. Look out! Same God, same purpose.

Secondly, he touches him in his hip breaking his natural strength. We cannot walk in the blessings of God relying on self! Paul found that out:

> *"We do not want you to be uninformed, brothers and sisters, about the troubles we experienced in the province of Asia. We were under great pressure, far beyond our ability to endure, so that we despaired of life itself. Indeed, we felt we had*

received the sentence of death. But this happened that we might not rely on ourselves but on God, who raises the dead. " 2 Corinthians 1:8-9.

No self-reliance needed!

Next Jacob tries to dissuade him asking, *"Let me go it is daybreak."*. Just like Elijah asked Elisha, *"Stay here!"*.

Jacobs' answer shows his determination! *"I will not let you go until you bless me!"*, was his cry. How hungry are we to walk in Gods' blessing? How determined to walk in our destiny? The God of Jacob will wrestle with us in the same manner he wrestled with Jacob!

Now God goes after how Jacob sees himself and what he calls himself. Our greatest hindrance to our fulfillment of destiny is not seeing ourselves in Gods eyes.
"What is your name?" he asks.
"Jacob" is the reply. His name meant *trickster* and *cheat*, *"NO IT'S NOT!"*, was the reply. That is how you see you, not how the Lord sees you. *"It is Israel!"* YOU ARE A PRINCE! You are a prevailer and man-affecter.... This is

why God came! He came to change Jacqbs view!!!!! Are we willing to let him change ours?

Now comes the blessing. After he changes his view and his reliance, *"Then he blessed him there."*. LOVE IT.

So, what was the determining factor? Jacob looked on his face and saw himself in God. THAT MY FRIENDS IS THE POWER OF A WRESTLE WITH GOD! Your destiny changes, you view changes and your walk changes.

Jacob limped out of the encounter but so carried the blessing of God that he was able to even minister that blessing to Pharaoh himself as well as his sons.

> *"Then Jacob blessed Pharaoh and went out from his presence."* Genesis 47:10

MY GOD, YOUR GOD

"The God of Jacob". You can't get more personal than that.
I love that statement by Darius to Daniel when cast into the
lion's den.

> *"Daniel, servant of the living God, has your God,*
> *whom you serve both day and night, been able to*
> *deliver you from the lions?"* Daniel 6:20.

Now listen to the answer,

> *"May the king live for ever! My God sent his angel,*
> *and he shut the mouths of the lions."* Daniel 6:21-22

Listen again, "Your God", "my God". There it is. This is
the God of Jacob and the God of Daniel. Now let's add a
few more to see how personal this is!

Abraham, in Genesis 17, receives a personal promise that
God would be "His God". That promise is referred to by
his servants in Genesis 24 more than once. In fact, the
servant uses it as his prayer base.

> *"Then he prayed, 'Lord, God of my master*
> *Abraham, make me successful today...'."*
> Genesis 24:12

Moses receives his promise in Deuteronomy 4:5.

Joshua receives his promise in Joshua 14:18

David continuously speaks of his promise, particularly in the Psalms.

And so many more!

Yes this God of Jacob, is a personal God, the God of Daniel and the God of Moses and Joshua. He is even introduced to us by Jesus in the Lord's Prayer. As

"Our father which art in Heaven…". Matt 6:10

But for scripture to be continually citing that he is the God of Jacob, we must grasp the significance of this relationship. God owns his relationship with you and you own your relationship with him. He lets it be known that he is your God! Surely then the God of Jacob can become my God!

Now let's add another dimension to this amazing relational statement. From the moment the Lord claims that his is "the God of", like Daniel, one finds out very quickly how it makes him act on behalf of those whom he claims. Look at Abraham and Isaac when a king goes after their wives. Then examine Daniel in the Lions' den. David was

continually protected from Saul and others. Add to that
Ezra who was protected by the hand of God and Moses
when Aaron and Miriam stood against him.

> *"But this is not true of my servant Moses; he is*
> *faithful in all my house. With him I speak face to*
> *face, clearly and not in riddles; he sees the form of*
> *the Lord. Why then were you not afraid to speak*
> *against my servant Moses?"* Numbers 12:7-8

That is a wow! When he takes ownership of the
relationship, that becomes more than heavy!

When we speak of the God of Jacob and us touching him,
knowing now that such a relationship is not just possible
but offered, it makes one want to be like Jacob and so
pursue him that in turn he becomes found of us. David
spoke of his passionate pursuit again and again and guess
what? He wrote of the God of Jacob multiple times and
taught his spiritual sons the same.

> *"Such is the generation that seek his face, your*
> *face, oh God of Jacob."* Psalm 24:6

There is our promise!!!

THE ONE WHO ANOINTS

David makes quite a profound statement

"...the man anointed by the God of Jacob."
2 Samuel 23:1

David's anointing was by the one who appeared to and ministered to Jacob. The God of Jacob is one who anoints! But what an anointing David was given! It is so historical. He was anointed in power, might and strength and as a psalmist in 1 Samuel 16:18, and again as a psalmist in 2 Samuel 23:1. He was anointed to be the King, to walk in authority in 1 Samuel 16:13 and as a prophet as seen by so many of his revelations and confirmed in Acts 2:30.

Touching the God of Jacob can never leave us the same person afterwards. Jacob himself came out another man from such a touch. If we, like David and according to Psalm 24:6, have any kind of face to face we will be forever changed!

Why does it matter that we can be anointed by the God of Jacob? It matters because, like Jacob and David, he anoints the ordinary and causes them to become extraordinary. David, the eighth born and quite rejected brother who was not even invited to the feast when Samuel arrives at his father's home, is anointed in front of his brothers and what he becomes is historical and eye opening. This is not just recorded in the Bible but in modern days there have been folks like Smith Wigglesworth, Bennie Hinn and Kathryn Kuhlman who were quite normal and ordinary but became anointed by the God of Jacob... the list could go on.

The Song of Solomon has a beautiful description of running into this anointer! It says his kiss is life changing and his name is like anointing poured out. There is the encounter! But it also says, "Pleasing are the fragrances of your perfume", or anointings. The ordinary girl from the vineyard was anointed by the God of Jacob.

The realms of anointing by God are profound but the moment we mention the God of Jacob it becomes such a personal encounter that it brings us out both anointed but also with a new knowing of God. To carry a touch of God is one thing but to know the God of the touch is another! Such is the promise when the God of Jacob encounters us and anoints us.

Anointing has so much to do with what we carry as a result. We are anointed to God and by God but anointed by the one who becomes so personal. We carry this anointing on his behalf. Watch this different statement: "Anointed by God!" Now try this: "Anointed by the God of Jacob!" It carries another meaning or significance.

I know for me that I love to carry the touch and anointing of the Lord, but seek a so much more significant anointing by knowing face to face my anointer.

THE EVER-PRESENT HELP IN TIMES OF TROUBLE

Psalm 46 is written by the sons of Korah. They are Levites but part of David's worship team and clearly affected by his walk with God and his *Tabernacle of David* worship. They pen a prophetic psalm of great significance. It's a psalm concerning the present help of God, his presence and protection and where we are encouraged to know him and his ever-flowing spirit. It is a psalm where The God of Jacob is mentioned twice.

> *"The Lord of hosts is with us; the God of Jacob is our refuge."* Repeated in Psalm 46:7 and 11

This statement was repeated in both verses, which of course established the truth by its double mention. Literally, he is a very present help in times of trouble.

> *"God is our refuge and strength, an ever-present help in trouble."* Psalm 46:1

But they were not saying this is an abstract statement that they had read about him but rather from a personal experience. "He is with us!" The sons of Korah, like David, had come into an encounter with this same God of Jacob. This is what they found out about him:

- He is always present. His *I am* presence can be known and experienced:

  "He says, "Be still, and know that I am God; I will be exalted among the nations, I will be exalted in the earth." Psalm 46:10

- He is there as a refuge and help.

- His river ministers to his people:

  "There is a river whose streams make glad the city of God, the holy place where the Most High dwells." Psalm 46:4

- He makes his people glad when his river touches them.

- We don't have to fight for ourselves, he fights for us. Hence, *"Be still and know that I am God."*

This adds another realm of excitement! The God of Jacob, the God of David and others mentioned, but now the God of the sons of Korah. This is the less known but not less significant. The sons of Korah were worshippers, servants and dedicated to the Lord. He is not just the God of the big named but those who equally seek his face! The God who is no respecter of persons:

"Then Peter opened his mouth, and said, of a truth I perceive that God is no respecter of persons." Acts 10:34 KJV

But what amazing benefits he brings! None other than the *I Am* presence of God! None other than the Psalm 91 promise of protection and being a refuge. Then add the ministry of the Holy Spirit, too. No wonder the Sons of Korah had to pen such a psalm and such a significant promise that they had experienced. One can only imagine the thrill they had when David revealed his own encounters but then when they found it was true for them and for all. It reminds me of the Song of Solomon:

> *"No wonder the maidens love you!"* Song of
> Solomon 1:3 NIV 1984 version

We have heard about it but now we have tasted it for ourselves! These, by the way, are the same Sons of Korah who penned this call:

> *"Deep calls to deep in the roar of your waterfalls;*
> *all your waves and breakers have swept over me."*
> Psalm 42:7

Surely the God of Jacob revelation is the deep calling to the deep! Sounding out there is MORE!

MAKING HIMSELF KNOWN TO JACOB

I have often made this statement while ministering, *"Desire belongs to us but encounter belongs to him. ".* What do I mean by that? Clearly, as previously stated, God stirs desire in us but what we do with that desire makes all the difference. The key to this chapter and perhaps the whole book is that God places that desire in us because he knows our response. He knew what Elisha would do and David would do and of course knew what Jacob would do. The God of Jacob wanted to make himself known to Jacob and thus become *His God.* THE GOD OF JACOB IS THE ONE WHO MAKES HIMSELF KNOWN! To become known as the God of Jacob, he had to make himself known to Jacob. For us to know this God of Jacob, he must reveal himself to us in the same manner.

Clearly, the Lord also reveals himself to others which is why David and others pick up on this name. How he reveals himself to Jacob is particularly important to us as we pursue our desire to touch this God of Jacob.

Firstly, Jacob saw God's relationship with his Grandfather Abraham and his father Isaac. Their accounts of his visitations must have stirred him greatly! Then his first personal encounter in Genesis 28:12-22 became to him, in his own words, *"Awesome"*. The Lord reveals himself at the top of a stairway:

> *"He had a dream in which he saw a stairway resting on the earth, with its top reaching to heaven, and the angels of God were ascending and descending on it.* **¹³** *There above it*[c] *stood the LORD, and he said: "I am the LORD, the God of your father Abraham and the God of Isaac."*
> Genesis 28:12-13

After all the accounts we had mentioned by his father and Grandfather, this was the perfect introduction. But how God came to Jacob is quite fascinating. Jacob himself says,

> *"How awesome is this place! This is none other than the house of God; this is the gate of heaven."*
> Genesis 28:17

The Lord had opened a porthole to visit him. God had brought heaven to Jacob's earth! This is the God of Jacob. He brought heaven to earth through Jesus, the outpouring of the Spirit and wants to bring heaven to your earth. God of Jacob, your kingdom come!

Jacob received dreams from the Lord, too, but it is his encounter in Genesis 32 that becomes the highlight of his encounters. It was not the first and not the last but clearly the highlight. Why? Because God allows him to see him face to face! This encounter changes him forever. He walks with a limp from it. It is where his father's God and his grandfather's God become his God. So much so, that from that time on the statement *the God of Jacob* becomes a corner stone of revelation brought to us by David himself and his sons in the Lord. When did David encounter the God of Jacob himself? Perhaps only heaven will reveal the moment, but the revelation was now upon him clearly as he says,

> *"The Lord said to my lord...."* Psalm 110:1

David later makes this statement:

> *"You make known to me the path of life; you will fill me with joy in your presence, with eternal pleasures at your right hand."* Psalm 16:11

This revelation of *The God of Jacob* is clearly one of these paths that David brought to us.

Remember this statement as we close this chapter: *THE GOD OF JACOB IS THE ONE WHO MAKES HIMSELF KNOWN!* Will it be the same way as it was to Jacob? Only he knows how and in which way but if you so desire, he so wants to encounter you, too.

MINISTERING FROM JACOBS WELL

It was only when I discovered the God of Jacob in such an awesome way that it suddenly dawned on me that the incredible miracle of John Chapter 4 was in fact right next to Jacobs well. It says,

> *"Jacob's well was there, and Jesus, tired as he was from the journey, sat down by the well. It was about noon."* John 4:6

The whole discourse and miracle of evangelism that occurred was right next to Jacobs well. That well was named Jacob's well because he dug it and drank from it and even, according to the context, gave the whole parcel of land including the well to Joseph his son:

> *"Now he had to go through Samaria. So he came to a town in Samaria called Sychar, near the plot of ground Jacob had given to his son Joseph."*
> John 4:4

Firstly, we have no record in the Old Testament of Jacob digging this well but hardly surprising when watching the history of his father and grandfather. But guess who did have a record of who dug this well? None other than the

God of Jacob! Jesus sits down next to it. Jesus ministers from it! What does this mean? It means that the God of Jacob misses nothing you do and whatever you gain in him, he uses it to minister to others from. Jacob did not know when he dug this well that the Lord would use it so greatly.

Secondly the God of Jacob, though greater than Jacob, would still allow Jacob to get the glory from something he did years before. He was asked,

> *"Are you greater than our father Jacob?"*
> John 4:12

I think so!!! I am using what he did to minister to others as my basis!

But thirdly, from the premise of the encounter with Jacob at his well he would offer the same encounter to not only a Samaritan woman but multitudes! The God of Jacob not only offered the same encounter in the Old Testament but now he offered it to the new generation as was prophesied:

> *"Such is the generation of those who seek him, who seek your face, God of Jacob."* Psalm 24:6

The context speaks of the father seeking the true worshippers:

> *"Yet a time is coming and has now come when the true worshipers will worship the Father in the Spirit and in truth, for they are the kind of worshipers the Father seeks. God is spirit, and his worshipers must worship in the Spirit and in truth."*
> John 4:23-24

Where more fitting than at the well dug by the worshipper who touched the heart of God...the worshipper who had a change of heart and destiny and had a change of name?

Now check the promises to the believers! The promise was given of a new heart, new garments and a new name. Prophesy is filled by it. The God of Jacob indeed remembers his covenants and from our encounters ministers to many.

What wells have we dug? What overflow of his life has poured into us and flows out from us? What have we touched that this God of Jacob could minister to others from? It was stated earlier that Jesus said that out of our bellies would flow streams and rivers of living waters.

How? It's ours by touching the same life giver as Jacob did. He owns the encounter and owns the relationship and looks to bless others from his touch on our lives!

Welcome, oh God of Jacob! We will not let you go, until you bless us.

WHEN THE GOD OF JACOB BECOMES THE GOD OF ISRAEL

It was previously mentioned that one of the greatest events of Jacob's life was his wrestle with God. The wrestle was started by God to produce the new man with the new name and the new walk. The whole event proves to us that God takes us in our worst state to produce a man or woman of influence. ISRAEL, one who prevails with God and prevails with man. Clearly he was a man of influence. The God of Jacob is the God of Israel!

This event was actually the destiny that Jacob wrestled with in the womb, as a young man and through his life until the God of Jacob released the full destiny of God into Jacob's life! We must become excited and stirred by this! The Lord will not leave you where you are but has a greater destiny for you. He has a destiny for you with a new name and place of influence in which you can walk. We are all called into this place where we can touch our destiny, we are all called into this place where, as New Testament priests, we can prevail on our God like Abraham did and Jacob did. From this place we can walk in a place of influence with men.

Let's follow the Israel experience.

- Destiny is dropped into a man's heart.
- Passion is stirred to follow the cry within him
- A desire to possess the blessing ensues. This of course can be seen with the dealings with Esau.
- A prevailing on God to release his destiny brings the Lord into face to face encounter.
- A wrestle with God that produces the new man.
- A face to face encounter to see who gives the promise and the anointing of the new.
- A breaking of the strength of the flesh as the hip is disjointed
- A pronouncing of the new name
- A blessing to walk in from that day.

All of this and more can be seen as God prepares him from birth to encounter in Genesis 25 through 32.

But we must walk in the new, not just gain it!

"God said to him, 'Your name is Jacob, but you will no longer be called Jacob; your name will be Israel.' So he named him Israel." Genesis 35:10

SO HE NAMED HIM ISRAEL! This is three chapters later and how many years? He had been told what he had gained but clearly would not walk in the fullness of it so the God of Jacob revealed a second time, *"but I am also the God of Israel"*! He named him Israel. He changed his name and would not let him any more walk in the old!

Abram became Abraham. Jacob becomes Israel. What new name and new places in God are available to those who avail themselves of such a relationship with the God of Jacob? This is found twice in the letters to the churches in Rev 2:17 and Rev 3:12. This is the promise to the generation of those that, like Jacob, seek his face as in Psalms 24:6.

AND HE BLESSED HIM THERE

What a great statement:

> *"Jacob said, 'Please tell me your name.' But he*
> *replied, 'Why do you ask my name:' Then he*
> *blessed him there."* Genesis 32:2

After the wrestle with God and the new name is given what Jacob had longed for was granted. He blessed him there!

There is a promise of God that every believer should take hold of found in Galatians:

> *"So those who have faith are blessed along with*
> *Abraham the man of faith,..."*
> Galatians 3:9 NIV 1984 version

I believe intensely that this was the blessing Jacob was after. He had seen it in his grandfather and had also seen it on his father Isaac…so much so that he even tricked him to get it. He wanted to walk in his Grandfather's blessing. The blessing of Abraham. We need to discover what we need to obtain it, because it is a promise to us, too, to be blessed alongside Abraham.

I think the great statement that we should look at is in the word, *there*. He blessed him *there*! Where? Because wherever that was I want to get *there* too! *There* is not a physical place but an encounter that brought the blessing. *There* is what brought the Lord from heaven to wrestle with Jacob. His intense longing, his refusal to give up, his place of ultimate weakness as his hip was touched by God and his face to face are all involved in this *there*. Perhaps this statement in verse 26 is the statement that everything hangs on: "I will not let you go until you bless me!" He is saying, "I know it belongs to me and I want it. I will not stop, whatever the cost, until I have that blessing that belongs to me." This my friends is what brings the blessing! Jabez also did this later in the Bible.

> *"Oh that you would bless me indeed,…"* 1
> Chronicles 4:9-10 KJV

The original language says, "Oh, that you would *Barak, Barak* me". You would *double portion bless me, with your blessing*! What? That is what Abraham had, the blessing that enabled Him to bless others.

> *"The LORD had said to Abram, "Go from your country, your people and your father's household to the land I will show you. I will make you into a*

great nation, and I will bless you; I will make your name great, and you will be a blessing. I will bless those who bless you, and whoever curses you I will curse; and all peoples on earth will be blessed through you.'" Genesis 12:1-3.

In fact, it is a blessing that blesses God himself and then his blessing overflows in blessing to others.

This God of Jacob who was persuaded by Jacob to bless him like Abraham is also our God, who promises to bless us alongside Abraham. It takes faith to believe he will because he wants to, faith to believe he wants to keep his word and persistence that will not let go until he does. Jacob did not worry about his issues. He worried about getting what was in his destiny. God dealt with the issues as he always will. Do we want our blessing, too?

Recall once again that Psalm 24:6, says, "...such is the generation that seek his face, your face oh God of Jacob." What for? To walk in is blessing! I am part of that special generation! You are, too! Seek his blessing we must, we should and we shall! I have noticed in my own life that it is the persistent seeking of God on his promises that seems to move him so intensely. The encounters that he has blessed me with seem to always have much of this Jacob factor in it. It seems that when, by the Holy Spirit's Grace, we pray in such a fashion, both heaven and earth are sounding the same sound.

> *"And the blessing of God that makes rich soon comes."* Proverbs 10:22

I WILL NOT LET YOU GO UNTIL, OH GOD OF JACOB, YOU BLESS ME, TOO!

CONCLUSION

This book touching the God of Jacob is an ongoing revelation for those who are hungry for more of God. Jacob watched the God of Abraham and Isaac and would soon join himself to the ranks. Yet more, he so touched God that the Lord gave him his own chapter as it were in the whole story of our patriarchs. One who came from behind in the natural and so touched God that God touched him. He walked with that touch the rest of his life.

It is a story that caused David to realize what could be found in God. David, who himself came from a non-privileged position, was caused to touch and carry the touch of God. In Psalm 24:6 he then went on to share his huge prophetic insight that this was going to be something that the next generation of the church could have available to them. We are in that generation.

Touching the God of Jacob shows a God who can be touched and will change the destiny of any that will access him. I am excited to share this revelation with you, praying that it will stir your heart like it has mine to want more and desire more and press in for more!

The cry of Jabez once again comes to mind: *"Oh that you would bless me."* The answer? Yes, I will! I AM THE GOD OF JACOB.

TESTIMONIAL

"I can confidently say that in 26 years of sitting under the ministry of Dennis Goldsworthy-Davis the revelation of The God of Jacob *is by far one of the most profound and life-changing messages I've ever experienced. The revelation is raw, real and hope filled as you learn of a man who refused anything but the blessing of God in his life. This revelation challenges us to believe that we can be a prince with God no matter our background or short-comings. As Dennis released this message in our local assembly the Presence of God tangibly testified to the truth of its revelation. I know, for one, my heart and life have been changed due to this revelation and I know yours will be, too." Chris Rodes, Great Grace International Christian Center*

BIOGRAPHY

Dennis Paul Goldsworthy-Davis has been blessed to travel extensively throughout the world ministering both apostolically and prophetically to the body of Christ. He operates within a strong governmental prophetic office and frequently sees the Presence of God and the Spirit of Revival break out upon the lives of people. Dennis has equally been graced to relate to many spiritual sons throughout the earth, bringing wisdom, guidance and encouragement.

Born in Southern Ireland and raised in England, Dennis was radically saved from a life of drugs and violence in 1973. Soon after his conversion, he began to operate within his local church where he was fathered spiritually by Bennie Finch, a seasoned apostolic minister. After working in youth ministry Dennis pastored in several areas within the U.K. It was during these pastorates that Dennis began to see profound moves of God in these same venues.

In 1986 Dennis experienced a dramatic shift in his life and ministry. He and his family moved to San Antonio, Texas, to join a vibrant, functioning apostolic team. In 1990 Dennis was commissioned to start Great Grace

International Christian Center, a local work in San Antonio. Dennis continues to serve as the Senior /Minister of GGICC and heads the formation of the apostolic team in the local house. Presently, Dennis relates to several functioning apostolic ministries. He draws wisdom and accountability from Robert Henderson of Global Reformers, Barry Wissler of HarvestNet International and for many years before his passing, Alan Vincent. Each of these carry strong, well-seasoned apostolic offices in their own right.

Dennis has been married to his wife Christine since 1973 and has two wonderful daughters and four grandchildren.

Made in the USA
Monee, IL
17 January 2021